# NUMBERS THAT PROPHESY OFFICIAL WORKBOOK

## HEARING GOD THROUGH HISTORIC HEADLINES AND NUMBERS THAT PREACH

TROY A. BREWER

DESTINY IMAGE

Destiny Image P.O. Box 310, Shippensburg, PA 17257-0310

This book and all other Destiny Image's books are available at Christian bookstores and distributors worldwide.

For Worldwide Distribution.

Reach us on the Internet: www.destinyimage.com.

ISBN 13 TP: 979-8-8815-0413-7

ISBN 13 eBook: 979-8-8815-0414-4

# CONTENTS

# INTRODUCTION

Welcome to "Numbers that Prophesy: Official Workbook," a transformative guide designed to deepen your understanding of the biblical significance of numbers and their prophetic meanings. This workbook is crafted to accompany you on a journey through the Scriptures, exploring how numbers reveal God's meticulous design and His messages to humanity throughout history.

From Genesis to Revelation, numbers weave a divine narrative that speaks to God's sovereignty, precision, and deep involvement in the world. Each chapter in this workbook is carefully designed to unpack these themes, providing you with a comprehensive view of how biblical numerology plays a pivotal role in understanding God's word and His promises to us.

KEY TAKEAWAYS FROM THIS WORKBOOK

- **Understanding Divine Patterns**: You will learn to identify and understand the repetitive numerical patterns throughout the Bible. These patterns are not coincidental but are purposefully placed by God to signify key theological truths, such as completeness, order, and perfection.

- **Deepening Biblical Literacy**: This workbook is designed to increase your biblical literacy by providing detailed explanations of how numbers are used in different scriptural contexts. By understanding these contexts, you can gain deeper insights into the narratives and teachings of the Bible.

- **Enhancing Spiritual Perception**: As you progress through this workbook, you will develop a heightened perception of how God communicates through numbers. This will not only enhance your spiritual discernment but will also encourage you to seek and recognize God's voice in your daily life.

- **Personal and Collective Growth**: The reflective questions and journaling prompts included in each chapter are intended to foster both personal reflection and community discussion. This approach ensures that the knowledge gained is not just theoretical but also applicable in personal and communal settings.

- **Encountering God in Everyday Life**: By integrating the prophetic insights from this workbook into your daily life, you will begin to see how God's messages are woven into the fabric of your everyday experiences. This realization will encourage a more mindful and spiritually attuned way of living.

## WHAT YOU CAN EXPECT TO RECEIVE

- **A Richer Understanding of Scripture**: Delve into the layers of meaning behind biblical stories and prophecies. This workbook will equip you with the tools to understand and interpret the significance of numbers found throughout the Scriptures.
- **Practical Applications**: Each chapter provides actionable steps to apply the knowledge gained. Whether you are a new believer or a seasoned scholar, these practical applications will help you to live out the truths discovered in your study.
- **Community and Fellowship**: Engage with a community of learners who are also exploring these truths. The discussion points and group activities are designed to foster a supportive learning environment, where insights can be shared and growth can be nurtured collectively.
- **Continual Spiritual Growth**: This workbook is designed to be a resource that you can return to time and again. The timeless nature of its content means that each read-through can offer new revelations and deeper understanding, depending on your spiritual journey at the time.
- **A Deeper Connection with God**: Ultimately, the greatest gift this workbook offers is a deeper, more intimate relationship with God. By understanding and appreciating the depth of His Word, you will grow closer to Him, enhancing your spiritual life and deepening your faith.

As we embark on this journey together, I invite you to open your heart and mind to the profound teachings that await. The numbers in Scripture are a gateway to understanding more about God's character and His incredible plan for your life. Embrace this opportunity to explore, learn, and grow. Your spiritual journey is about to get richer, and I am thrilled to guide you through every step of the way.

~

# CHAPTER 1

# PROPHETIC HISTORIC EVENT 1- PRESIDENT LINCOLN AND THE CIVIL WAR

Remember, even in tumultuous times, God's hand can be discerned, guiding and shaping the course of history. Challenges and crises often precede significant transformations and are laden with lessons and opportunities for growth.

**"For My thoughts are not your thoughts, nor are your ways My ways," says the Lord. "For as the heavens are higher than the earth, so are My ways higher than your ways, and My thoughts than your thoughts." (Isaiah 55:8-9 NKJV)**

In the chapter we explore, one remarkable aspect that stands out is President **Lincoln's Prophetic Dream** where he foresaw his own demise. This dream wasn't just a fleeting nightmare; it was imbued with significance, showing us how deeply interconnected personal destiny can be with the fate of a nation. As I recount this, it's not merely to add a mystical layer to Lincoln's story but to underscore the burden of leadership and prophetic insight that he carried. His dream acted as a somber reflection of the enormous responsibilities and the profound anxieties that shaped his presidency.

As we delve deeper into the symbolism surrounding his assassination, we uncover the **Significance of Timing and Numbers**. The events of Lincoln's death aligned with Passover and Good Friday, which are pivotal moments in biblical narratives of sacrifice and deliverance. This alignment isn't coincidental but rather seems to elevate the historical moment, suggesting a divine orchestration at play. Here, we see the profound layers of meaning that can emerge when we consider the symbolic weight of specific dates and numerical details associated with such a pivotal event.

The **Impact of Lincoln's Policies**, notably the Emancipation Proclamation and the push for the 13th Amendment, were monumental. These actions didn't just reshape the political landscape of America—they were spiritually emblematic, mirroring the biblical deliverance narratives. Lincoln, through his leadership, not only fought a civil war but also waged a moral battle to end slavery, positioning himself as a modern-day Moses or deliverer in the eyes of many.

In exploring the names and dates associated with Lincoln and his time, we tap into the **Symbolism in Names and Dates**. Lincoln's own name, suggesting "lives by the water," and those of his contemporaries carry deep symbolic meanings that resonate with biblical themes. These names and dates aren't just historical footnotes; they are laden with prophetic significance, offering us insights into the deeper narrative God might be weaving through our history.

The broader impact of the Civil War is a profound theme in this discussion. The **The Civil War's Broader Impact** on America was both devastating and transformative, altering the nation's psyche and demographic structure. This war wasn't just a battle over territory or governance but a significant societal upheaval that fundamentally changed the United States.

Understanding historical events through a **The Role of Prophetic Interpretation** invites us to see beyond the mere facts of history to the divine messages possibly encoded within. This approach doesn't undermine the historical record but enriches our understanding by integrating spiritual discernment, which can reveal deeper truths and lessons from our past.

The **Cultural and Historical Context** in which the Civil War occurred adds layers to our understanding of the conflict. This context helps us appreciate the varied motivations and perspectives of those involved. Recognizing that the war, to many, was about states' rights or economic structures, and not initially about slavery, adds complexity to our understanding of this pivotal period.

Lincoln's unique vision and steadfast leadership are highlighted in **Lincoln's Vision and Leadership**. His commitment to justice and equality, his use of prophetic dreams, and his moral courage were all elements that defined his presidency. These traits not only made him a notable leader but also a prophetic figure, akin to those found in Scripture, who are called for a divine purpose.

The interpretation of dreams and visions, as seen in **Interpretation of Dreams and Visions**, was significant not only for Lincoln but can be for us as well. Lincoln's recurring dreams, which seemed to foreshadow major events or decisions, highlight the prophetic nature of his leadership. These weren't just idle visions but were imbued with meaning, urging him toward his historic and moral objectives.

Lastly, the **Lasting Legacy and Prophetic Significance** of Abraham Lincoln's life and presidency remind us that our leaders can be seen as fulfilling divine purposes. Lincoln's story is not just one of political acumen but also of a higher calling, where his actions and decisions resonate with the biblical themes of liberation and divine destiny.

As we journey through this chapter, I invite you to see these events not just as historical facts but as moments filled with divine intention and prophetic significance. Each aspect of Lincoln's story and the Civil War holds lessons and meanings that go beyond the battlefield, reaching into the very soul of America.

### REFLECTIVE QUESTIONS

1. How do the symbolic interpretations of names and dates enhance our understanding of historical events like Lincoln's assassination?
2. In what ways do Lincoln's prophetic dreams reflect the challenges and responsibilities of leadership?
3. What lessons can we draw from the intersection of significant historical events and their alignment with biblical themes of sacrifice and deliverance?
4. How does considering the Civil War through a prophetic lens change our perception of its causes and consequences?
5. What implications does the concept of divine orchestration have for our understanding of personal and national destiny?

### ACTIONABLE STEPS

- **Cultivate an Understanding of Prophetic Symbols:** Enhance your ability to recognize and interpret prophetic symbols in daily life by studying biblical symbolism and its historical contexts.

- **Equip with Historical Knowledge**: Deepen your understanding of significant historical events like the Civil War by exploring diverse sources and perspectives to appreciate the complexity of historical narratives.
- **Engage in Reflective Journaling**: Regularly journal about how current events and personal experiences might be understood from a prophetic perspective, considering what lessons they might teach about divine patterns and purposes.

JOURNALING **Prompt**

Reflect on a recent personal or global event that troubled or confused you. How might viewing this event through a prophetic lens change your understanding of its significance and your response to it?

～

# CHAPTER 2

# PROPHETIC HISTORIC EVENT 2 - THE RMS TITANIC

Let us remember that in our most challenging times, we are never forsaken. God's promise is to be with us, to guide us through the storms. We need only to listen and trust in His guidance.

**The Lord will guide you continually, and satisfy your soul in drought, and strengthen your bones; You shall be like a watered garden, and like a spring of water, whose waters do not fail. - Isaiah 58:11 NKJV**

As we delve into the historical and prophetic significance of the Titanic's tragic voyage, it becomes clear that the events surrounding its sinking are more than mere coincidences. These events serve as divine markers, revealing deeper spiritual lessons and warnings. The **Prophetic Alignments of Dates** between the assassination of President Lincoln and the sinking of the Titanic underline a mysterious, divine orchestration of history. Both events happened from April 14 to April 15, separated by years, yet interconnected by a thread of prophetic insight, suggesting that God speaks through significant dates to convey spiritual truths.

In pondering the downfall of the Titanic, likened to the biblical fall of Babylon, we're reminded of the dangers of pride and self-glorification. The scriptures in Isaiah 47 draw a parallel that is impossible to ignore, pointing to the **Symbolic Interpretations of Tragedy**. The Titanic, much like ancient Babylon, was a symbol of peak human achievement and opulence, yet it was not immune to disaster. This serves as a stark reminder that without acknowledging God's sovereignty, even the greatest human achievements are vulnerable and can lead to downfall.

Throughout its journey, the Titanic received multiple warnings about the iceberg-laden path ahead. The decision to ignore these warnings resulted in catastrophe. This illustrates a vital lesson on the importance of **Warnings Ignored**. It's crucial for us as leaders, in whatever capacity we serve, to heed warnings— both divine and practical. Ignoring such advisements can lead to irreversible consequences, just as it did with the Titanic.

The story of the Titanic is also a narrative enriched by **The Power of Prophetic Voices**. Individuals like W.T. Stead and Morgan Robertson had penned predictions that eerily foretold the disaster. Their writings weren't mere coincidences but were imbued with prophetic insight, serving as a warning to all who would listen. This teaches us the value of recognizing and heeding the prophetic voices God places in our lives, as they often carry warnings meant to guide us towards safety and God's will.

Moreover, the Titanic's reliance on the pinnacle of **Spiritual Symbolism in Technology and Progress** at the time, such as its state-of-the-art construction and the Marconi wireless system, serves as a cautionary tale. It shows that technological advancements and human ingenuity, while valuable, cannot replace divine wisdom and protection. Our achievements must be coupled with humility and a recognition of our dependence on God.

The Titanic's fate was also shaped by the actions of its leaders. The **Role of Leadership in Heeding Warnings** is a critical takeaway. Leaders have the responsibility to listen to warnings, discern wisely, and act prudently to avert disaster. This underscores the broader biblical principle that wise leadership involves humility, consultation, and a readiness to alter course when necessary.

Divine protection often manifests most strikingly through stories of near misses. **Divine Protection for the Obedient** is evident in the accounts of notable individuals who were meant to be on the Titanic but were not. Their stories, from John Mott to Guglielmo Marconi, demonstrate how obedience to God's subtle nudgings can spare us from harm. These instances encourage us to seek and follow divine guidance diligently.

In the aftermath of the sinking, a reflection on **Repentance and Redemption** emerges. The Titanic serves as a metaphor for repentance, calling us to turn away from our pride and self-sufficiency to seek redemption through Christ. Just as the Titanic's passengers faced a literal call to abandon ship, we too are called to abandon our sinful ways and turn towards God's saving grace.

This historical event also challenges us to maintain an **Eternal Perspective on Temporary Glories**. The Titanic, once deemed unsinkable, now rests at the bottom of the ocean, a sobering reminder of the fleeting nature of earthly glories. This compels us to focus on eternal truths and the lasting kingdom of God, rather than the temporary triumphs of this world.

Lastly, the narrative of the Titanic is imbued with **The Importance of Heeding Prophetic Insights**. The disaster not only serves as a historical account of a maritime tragedy but also as a prophetic allegory, warning us of the perils of ignoring divine guidance. Just as the Titanic was ill-prepared for its encounter with an iceberg, we too can be unprepared for life's challenges if we disregard the prophetic insights that God provides through His word and His servants.

Through the lens of the Titanic's story, we are reminded of the importance of humility, the necessity of heeding divine warnings, and the power of prophetic insight. Let us take these lessons to heart, allowing them to guide us in our daily lives and spiritual journeys.

### Reflective Questions

1. How can we better attune ourselves to recognize and heed the prophetic warnings in our own lives?
2. What lessons can we learn about pride and humility from the story of the Titanic?
3. In what ways does this chapter challenge your understanding of divine protection and intervention?
4. How does the story of the Titanic encourage you to place greater value on eternal rather than temporal achievements?
5. What steps can you take to ensure that you are not ignoring God's voice in pursuit of your own goals?

### Actionable Steps

- **Cultivate a Heart of Obedience**: Commit to daily prayer and scripture reading to cultivate a heart that is receptive to God's warnings and guidance.
- **Equip Yourself with Knowledge**: Study historical and biblical instances of prophetic fulfillment to

equip yourself with the understanding needed to discern God's voice in your life.

- **Engage in Community Discernment**: Actively engage in your faith community to seek collective wisdom and accountability in interpreting and acting on prophetic insights.

JOURNALING **Prompt**

Reflect on a time when you felt like you ignored a warning (spiritual, practical, or both). What were the consequences, and what did you learn about the importance of obedience and discernment?

~

# CHAPTER 3

# PROPHETIC HISTORIC EVENT 3-"MAN" ON THE MOON

In the face of seemingly insurmountable challenges, we find our true capacity for greatness, guided by faith and fortified by the knowledge that we are never alone in our endeavors. Whether venturing into unknown territories or facing the trials of life on Earth, the same truth holds: we can achieve the extraordinary under God's watchful eyes.

**Wherefore by their fruits ye shall know them.** (Matthew 7:20 KJV)

In reflecting on the monumental journey of Apollo 11, I am moved by the **Prophetic Alignments of Historical Events** that mark this mission as not only a technological triumph but a spiritually significant moment. When Bill Safire prepared a contingency speech for President Nixon, it highlighted a profound understanding of the risks involved—representing both human foresight and a divine safeguard against potential tragedy. This gesture resonated deeply with me, emphasizing the blend of human preparation and the unseen hand guiding and protecting us.

As we delve deeper into the events of the lunar landing, the **Power of Words Under Pressure** becomes evident. Neil Armstrong's legendary phrase, uttered as he made mankind's giant leap on the lunar surface, was meant to include the word "a" before "man." This slip, or perhaps divine intervention, broadened the statement from a singular to a collective achievement. It's a vivid reminder that our words, especially under pressure, can echo far beyond their intended scope, shaping perceptions and interpretations on a grand scale.

The mission itself was a blend of **Technological Triumphs and Human Courage**. Armstrong's calm and quick decision-making as the lunar module Eagle's fuel dwindled exemplifies the best of human bravery, underscored by a reliance on groundbreaking technology. It was through Armstrong's adept handling of this precarious situation that the mission avoided disaster, a scenario that profoundly illustrates how human courage complements technological advancements.

One cannot overlook the **Divine Protection in Critical Moments** throughout this mission. As alarms blared and the landscape of the moon approached at an alarming speed, the successful landing of Apollo 11's Eagle module could be seen as nothing short of miraculous. This incident serves as a powerful testament to the presence of divine oversight in moments of acute danger, where every second counts and the margin for error is slim.

The **Recognition of Prophetic Insights in Secular Achievements** in the moon landing is underscored by its alignment with biblical scriptures, particularly Matthew 7:20, "By their fruits ye shall know them." This scriptural reference at the moment of the lunar landing invites us to view these scientific achievements through a spiritual lens, recognizing that our endeavors might also fulfill divine prophecies or teachings.

In exploring the moon, humanity extended its reach beyond our earthly confines, symbolizing our innate desire to explore and transcend our known limits. The entire Apollo 11 mission stands as a **Symbolic Representation of Human Endeavors**, challenging us to pursue our dreams, however daunting they may be, with tenacity and courage.

The physical and **Spiritual Lessons from Physical Challenges** encountered, such as the potentially explosive lunar dust, also speak volumes. These challenges not only tested the astronauts' resolve but also pointed to the broader spiritual lessons about the frailty and resilience of human life and our endeavors.

**The Role of Unity in Collective Success** was vividly demonstrated by the Apollo 11 team. Armstrong, Aldrin, and Collins worked seamlessly together to achieve what had once seemed an impossible feat. This unity mirrors the spiritual principle that collective human efforts, guided by divine wisdom, can achieve monumental goals.

The mission was also rich in **Historical and Prophetic Numbers**, which offer a deeper understanding of its spiritual significance. The recurrence of numbers like 6 and 11 not only marked this mission historically but also aligned it with biblical themes, suggesting a divine structure and purpose behind these human achievements.

Finally, the **Enduring Impact on Human Consciousness** of Apollo 11's mission cannot be understated. This event expanded our perceptions of what is possible, encouraging future generations to continue pushing the boundaries of what we can achieve, both physically and spiritually. As we reflect on this mission, we are reminded of our potential to not only explore new worlds but to also delve into the deeper meanings of our actions and their alignments with a higher purpose.

As we journey together through this narrative, I invite you to ponder these reflections and consider how the divine might be guiding your own explorations and achievements.

**REFLECTIVE QUESTIONS**

1. What personal 'moonshots' are you aiming for in your life, and how does your faith guide your pursuit?
2. How can you apply the lesson of 'Power of Words Under Pressure' in your everyday challenges?
3. In what ways can you demonstrate 'Technological Triumphs and Human Courage' in your community or workplace?
4. Reflect on a time when you felt 'Divine Protection in Critical Moments.' How did that experience shape your view of God's role in your life?
5. How can the 'Enduring Impact on Human Consciousness' of a historical event inspire you to leave a lasting legacy?

**ACTIONABLE STEPS**

- **Cultivate** an attitude of resilience and adaptability. Just as the Apollo 11 team demonstrated immense flexibility and courage in the face of unforeseen challenges, strive to develop these qualities in your personal and professional life.
- **Equip** yourself with knowledge and skills that align with your goals. Whether it's technological expertise, like that demonstrated during the Apollo mission, or

spiritual wisdom, investing in your growth will prepare you for your 'moonshots.'
- **Engage** with your community to share the lessons learned from Apollo 11. Organize a community event or a discussion group where you can discuss the interplay of faith, courage, and technology, and inspire others to reach for their 'moon.'

JOURNALING **Prompt**

Reflect on the intersection of faith and ambition in your life. How does your spiritual belief system support or challenge your aspirations? Journal about how the Apollo 11 mission can serve as a metaphor for your personal and spiritual endeavors.

# CHAPTER 4

# PROPHETIC HISTORIC EVENT 4- THE SPACE SHUTTLE COLUMBIA

This tragedy is a solemn reminder of our vulnerability and a prophetic call to return to our spiritual priorities.

**Remember therefore from where you have fallen; repent and do the first works, or else I will come to you quickly and remove your lampstand from its place—unless you repent.**
(Revelation 2:5 NKJV)

Reflecting on the **Columbia disaster**, we confront the profound truths about human endeavors and divine warnings. The Space Shuttle Columbia tragedy, involving a crew led by a man who loved God deeply, represents not only a technological failure but also a spiritual message to us all. It forces us to consider the consequences of deviating from our foundational beliefs and commitments.

Rick Husband, a man at the pinnacle of his profession who loved God fervently, leads us to reflect on the **Interplay Between Professional Excellence and Spiritual Devotion**. His life reminds us that personal success does not shield us from the vulnerabilities of existence. Instead, it calls us to balance our professional pursuits with spiritual depth and commitment.

As we consider the Columbia crew—exceptional individuals in both their professional fields and personal character—we face the harsh reality of **Unexpected Disasters in Life**. Such events do not discriminate based on one's goodness or achievements. They serve as somber reminders that calamity can strike anyone, reinforcing the need for spiritual preparedness and perspective.

**The Role of Leadership in Times of Crisis** comes sharply into focus as we recount the actions taken during the mission's critical moments. The decisions made by NASA and the crew in the face of mounting dangers remind us of the heavy responsibilities that leaders bear. Their choices can have far-reaching implications, not just for them but for all under their stewardship.

In this historical moment, we also see a **Prophetic Message About National Complacency**. The Columbia disaster metaphorically speaks to nations, particularly the United States, about the dangers of overconfidence and neglect of foundational principles. It warns of the peril that comes when nations, like individuals, drift away from their 'first love'—the core values and spiritual commitments that define and protect them.

Through this event, we are called to recognize the **Significance of Prophetic Symbols in Everyday Events**. Just as the prophets of old used real-life occurrences to convey deeper spiritual truths, so too does this modern catastrophe offer symbolic insights. It prompts us to look beyond the surface and seek the spiritual lessons embedded within our life experiences.

Moreover, the Columbia tragedy underscores the **Universality of Human Experience**—the shared destiny of humanity in the face of life's unpredictability. It reminds us that regardless of our background, achievements, or spiritual beliefs, we are all subject to the same physical laws and ultimate fate.

This event also serves as a **Call to Spiritual Awakening**. It beckons us to examine our lives, correct our courses, and realign with our spiritual foundations. Just as the disaster was a wake-up call for the space exploration community to review and improve their protocols, it serves as a metaphor for us to spiritually reassess and renew.

Reflecting on the **Legacy of Those Who Perished**, we are inspired to live lives of purpose and impact. The crew of Columbia, in their pursuit of knowledge and exploration, exemplifies the human spirit's quest for understanding and improvement. Their legacy encourages us to pursue our missions with vigor and integrity.

Lastly, the **Enduring Hope Amidst Tragedy** shines through. Even in the aftermath of such a devastating event, the human spirit's resilience and the divine promises of restoration and redemption offer solace and hope. This tragedy, while marking an end, also points to new beginnings and the continuous cycle of learning, growth, and spiritual evolution.

As we journey through the memory and implications of this event, let us ponder these reflections and seek ways to incorporate their lessons into our lives.

### Reflective Questions

1. How can the balance between professional achievements and spiritual devotion be maintained in your life?
2. What measures can you take to prepare spiritually for unexpected disasters?
3. In what ways can you exercise responsible leadership in your community or workplace?
4. How can you ensure that your national or personal values remain aligned with your spiritual beliefs?

5. What steps can you take to awaken or reawaken your spiritual life in response to the lessons from the Columbia disaster?

## ACTIONABLE STEPS

- **Cultivate** a balanced approach to life that honors both your professional responsibilities and your spiritual health. Draw inspiration from Rick Husband's life to integrate faith into all aspects of your life.
- **Equip** yourself with the knowledge and spiritual tools needed to navigate life's unexpected challenges. Engage in regular spiritual practices that strengthen your faith and resilience.
- **Engage** in community leadership or support roles that allow you to influence positively and guide others during times of crisis or uncertainty, drawing on the lessons learned from the leadership during the Columbia mission.

## JOURNALING Prompt

Reflect on the legacy you wish to leave behind. How does the story of the Columbia crew inspire you to pursue your goals with a renewed sense of purpose and commitment to your spiritual values?

# CHAPTER 5

# PROPHETIC HISTORIC EVENT 5 - PRINCESS DIANA AND MOTHER TERESA

Let us draw inspiration from the lives of these two remarkable women to strive for greater dedication to service and love. Recognizing the power we have to affect change in the world can guide us to lead lives marked by love and meaningful action.

**"Let your light so shine before men, that they may see your good works and glorify your Father in heaven." - Matthew 5:16 NKJV**

In this exploration, we uncover the spiritual lessons embedded in the life and death of two extraordinary women, Princess Diana and Mother Teresa, whose lives and passings paint a vivid picture of the **Stark Contrast Between External Beauty and Internal Virtue**. While Princess Diana's life was a tragic tale of beauty haunted by the glaring flashes of paparazzi, Mother Teresa's existence exemplified a serene devotion, shunning the limelight for service in the shadows of society's forgotten corners. Through their stories, we are reminded that true fulfillment stems not from external adoration but from a life of purpose and service.

Turning to **The Impact of Media and Public Perception**, Princess Diana's experience reveals the harsh realities of living under the constant scrutiny of public and media eyes. Her life, paralleled by Mother Teresa's modest existence, challenges us to consider our own focus. Are we, too, caught in the pursuit of validation through visibility rather than through the quiet dignity of genuine acts of kindness?

This discourse leads us to ponder **The Role of Divine Calling in Guiding Life's Purpose**. Mother Teresa's unwavering commitment to the destitute and dying underlined her life's mission, dictated by a divine calling that she followed with unmatched fervor. In contrast, Diana's pursuits, though noble, were often overshadowed by the complexities and expectations of her royal life, prompting us to introspect our alignment with our spiritual or worldly callings.

Through the details of their demise, we recognize **The Prophetic Significance of Numbers and Events**. The tragic crash that ended Diana's life and the peaceful passing of Mother Teresa unfold profound spiritual narratives, signifying the undeniable voice of the divine through ordinary sequences and settings. Such symbolism encourages us to look deeper into the everyday, seeking the spiritual messages woven into our own lives.

Furthermore, the legacy of these women brings to light **The Universal Themes of Love and Service**. Diana, celebrated for her charitable works, and Teresa, for her sacrificial service, both embodied love in action. Their lives prompt us to reflect on how we might express these virtues more fully in our interactions and choices.

Moreover, Diana's life serves as a stark reminder of **The Warning Against Worldly Distractions**. Her high-profile existence, marked by personal struggles and public interest, underscores the peril of succumbing to the superficial lures of society. This warning calls us to anchor our lives in values that transcend temporal allure.

Contrastingly, Mother Teresa's life epitomizes **The Enduring Influence of Spiritual Commitment**. Her global impact, achieved without the pursuit of fame, exemplifies that the most profound influence is often wielded not through power or prestige but through the quiet strength of steadfast spiritual commitment.

The narrative of their ends, too, offers a moment for profound reflection on **Mortality and Eternal Legacy**. The way each life concluded brings us face-to-face with the inevitability of death and the question of what legacy we choose to leave behind—will it be one of worldly recognition or one of spiritual significance?

Both their stories collectively serve as **A Call to Spiritual Reflection and Action**. They beckon us to evaluate our existence against the backdrop of eternal truths, urging us to embrace a life of deeper spiritual engagement and altruistic action.

Finally, the convergence of their life lessons brings us to understand **The Need for a Return to First Loves**—a return to the essentials of spiritual devotion and service that both women, in their unique ways, exemplified. This reflection urges us to prioritize our spiritual commitments over material pursuits, guiding us back to the foundational values of our faith.

As we journey through this chapter, let us carry with us the profound lessons learned from the lives of these two iconic women. Let their legacies inspire us to lead lives that are not just remembered for their superficial successes but revered for their spiritual significance and service to humanity.

· · ·

### REFLECTIVE QUESTIONS

1. How does the public's perception of Princess Diana and Mother Teresa challenge our own values regarding fame and humility?
2. In reflecting on the 'Stark Contrast Between External Beauty and Internal Virtue,' what steps can we take to cultivate a life that prioritizes internal growth over external validation?
3. Considering the 'Role of Divine Calling,' how can we better discern and follow our own divine callings amidst the distractions of modern life?
4. What lessons can we learn from the 'Prophetic Significance of Numbers and Events' in the deaths of Diana and Teresa to apply to understanding events in our own lives?
5. How does the 'Need for a Return to First Loves' resonate with your current spiritual journey, and what adjustments are needed to realign with this foundational value?

### ACTIONABLE STEPS

- **Cultivate** a deeper understanding of your spiritual calling by dedicating time each week to solitude and prayer, focusing on what God may be directing you towards in this season of your life.
- **Equip** yourself with knowledge about the lives of those who have prioritized spiritual values over worldly success by reading biographies of spiritual

leaders such as Mother Teresa and others who have made significant impacts through humble service.

- **Engage** in acts of anonymous service in your community to practice humility and love without seeking recognition, reflecting the life of Mother Teresa.

**J**OURNALING **Prompt**

Reflect on the contrast between the lives of Princess Diana and Mother Teresa. How does this comparison inspire you to evaluate your own life choices and their alignment with your values? Write about ways you can incorporate lessons from their lives into your daily living to foster a legacy of love and service.

~

# CHAPTER 6

# PROPHETIC HISTORIC EVENT 6 - 9/11 TERRORIST ATTACKS ON THE UNITED STATES OF AMERICA

Let's embrace the message of redemption and renewal. Even amidst the deepest trials, there is a promise of revival and restoration, a reminder that God's presence brings the hope we need to rebuild and renew our spirits.

**"I will lift up my eyes to the hills—From whence comes my help? My help comes from the Lord, Who made heaven and earth." - Psalm 121:1-2 NKJV**

I n examining the **Prophetic Significance of the 9/11 Attacks**, we see that these events were not just moments of national tragedy, but also pivotal points of spiritual awakening. The profound unity and spiritual revival that swept through America in the aftermath highlight how, even in the darkest moments, there can be a powerful movement towards God.

Reflecting on **The Preparation and the Premonitions** given before the attacks, it becomes clear that God communicates with us even in times of impending crisis, preparing those attuned to

His voice to lead and offer solace in times of need. This preparation underscores the importance of being receptive to spiritual insights that can sometimes come long before they make sense.

The **Heroism and Sacrifice** displayed by first responders and ordinary citizens remind us of the profound capacity for humans to exhibit God's love through acts of courage and selflessness. These stories of valor and bravery are testimonies to the indomitable spirit crafted in God's image.

Considering the **Cultural and Global Impact**, the attacks on 9/11 reshaped global policies and the international response to terrorism and forged a new era of global solidarity against threats to humanity. This shift reminds us of our interconnectedness and the global implications of national events.

Through the **Symbolism of Ashes and Mourning** seen on that day, we are reminded of the biblical use of ashes as a symbol of mourning and repentance. This imagery calls us to a collective mourning for lost innocence and a move towards repentance and spiritual renewal.

The **Continuous Remembrance** of 9/11 through media and personal stories acts as a call to never forget the lessons learned and the lives lost. It challenges us to keep the memories alive as a way to honor those who perished and to continually learn from the past.

The **Prophetic Patterns and Numbers**, such as the significant use of the numbers 9 and 11, offer deeper insights into God's messages during these events. These patterns encourage us to seek out the spiritual meanings behind earthly occurrences.

In **The Role of the Church Post-9/11**, there is a clear call for the church to be a beacon of hope and healing. The revival that followed the attacks showed the church stepping up as a community of faith, providing support, guidance, and a reminder of divine sovereignty in trying times.

**The Importance of God's Protection** highlighted by these

events reminds us that our true security lies not in human measures but in the providential care of God. This invites us to lean more on our spiritual foundation than on physical securities.

Lastly, the **Promise of Revival and Restoration** reflects the biblical promise that God will bring good from the trials, and that revival in the hearts of His people can arise from the ashes of destruction. This promise encourages us to look forward with hope and faith in God's redemptive plans.

As we reflect on the events of 9/11, these key points guide us to a deeper understanding and a stronger faith, reminding us of the enduring presence of God even in the midst of calamity.

### REFLECTIVE QUESTIONS

1. How has the cultural and global impact of 9/11 affected your perspective on international relations and security?
2. What personal lessons about heroism and sacrifice have you learned from the stories of 9/11, and how do they influence your daily life?
3. Reflecting on the prophetic patterns and numbers, what insights can you draw about God's communication through events?
4. Considering the continuous remembrance of 9/11, how can we use this reflection to foster a community that values history and its lessons?
5. With the promise of revival and restoration, what steps can you take to contribute to spiritual renewal within your community?

### Actionable Steps

- **Cultivate** a deeper personal reflection on the events of 9/11 by visiting a memorial or participating in a remembrance service, to personally connect with the national mourning and the lessons it teaches.
- **Equip** yourself with knowledge about global security and interfaith relations to better understand the complexities of post-9/11 world dynamics and contribute to peace-building initiatives.
- **Engage** in community service or interfaith dialogue to embody the unity and collective healing that can emerge from tragic events, fostering an environment of mutual respect and understanding.

### Journaling Prompt

Reflect on where you were during the 9/11 attacks and how you processed the events. Write about how your understanding of God's presence during such times has evolved since then. Consider what changes you can make in your life to align more closely with the divine protection and peace God offers.

# CHAPTER 7
# THE HYPE OF TYPE

**Trust in the Lord with all your heart and lean not on your own understanding; in all your ways submit to him, and he will make your paths straight. Proverbs 3:5-6 NKJV**

As we explore the ways God communicates with us, it's essential to grasp the concept of **The Significance of Types and Shadows**. These biblical methods are not merely historical footnotes but are active, dynamic means through which God imparts wisdom and revelation. The Old Testament is replete with events and rituals that prefigure and illuminate New Testament truths. By studying these, we can perceive God's plans and purposes with greater clarity, helping us understand the continuity and depth of His word.

Another profound aspect of divine communication is through **Understanding Prophetic Symbols**. The Bible uses symbols extensively—each one laden with spiritual significance that transcends time and culture. Recognizing these symbols within Scripture and discerning their application in our lives can open up new dimensions of understanding God's messages to

His people. For instance, water often symbolizes life and cleansing, while fire can represent God's presence or His refining process.

In our journey through Scripture, we also encounter **The Role of Numbers in Divine Communication**. Biblical numerology is not about superstition; it's about understanding the embedded truths within God's word. Numbers like 40, 12, and 3 are repeated throughout the Bible with specific theological implications, pointing to concepts of completeness, government, and divine wholeness. Such insights enhance our appreciation for the meticulous detail and depth of God's communicative methods.

Our understanding deepens as we realize **God's Persistent Voice Through History**. God's methods of speaking are as eternal as His nature. By recalling how God spoke to the ancients, we can tune our ears to hear His voice today, ensuring we do not miss His current revelations. This historical continuity is not just about learning facts but about engaging with a living dialogue that spans generations.

**Modern Applications of Biblical Types** reveal that the stories of old are not locked in the past; they resonate with relevance in our present context. Understanding types like Joseph as a precursor to Christ, or Jonah's ordeal pointing to Jesus' resurrection, bridges our world with the biblical world, showing us that God's messages are timeless and ever-relevant.

Each divine message, while universally applicable, is intricately tailored for individual reception, which brings us to **The Personal Nature of God's Messages**. This personal approach shows God's intimate concern for each of us, affirming that He speaks into the specifics of our lives with precision and care. Every scripture, every parable, and every number holds a personal application that can guide, correct, or encourage us in our unique spiritual journeys.

However, the reception of these messages is often challenging due to **The Offensiveness of the Prophetic**. Prophetic truth can be confrontational, challenging our preconceptions and prompting us to repentance and deeper commitment. This is not for our discomfort but for our growth and refinement, pushing us towards a more authentic and powerful discipleship.

Understanding and responding to God's voice requires a specific posture; hence, **The Necessity of a Prophetic Posture** is vital. This posture is one of openness and readiness to act upon the revelations we receive, even when they come without full clarity of the immediate outcomes. Such a stance ensures that we are not merely hearers of the word but active participants in God's transformative work.

**Integration of Prophecy in Daily Life** involves recognizing that prophecy is not reserved for the 'spiritually elite' but is accessible to every believer. By integrating prophetic insights into our daily decisions, we enhance our life's spiritual dimension and our effectiveness in the kingdom of God.

Lastly, the foundation of all prophetic understanding is in **The Imperative of Remembering**. Recalling God's past faithfulness is crucial for sustaining our faith. It serves as a foundation for present belief and future hope. Remembering the deeds and promises of God anchors us in His faithfulness, empowering us to live with confidence and to pass on a legacy of faith.

These ten key points are not just theological constructs but are practical tools that can guide us in recognizing and responding to God's voice. By embracing these principles, we can live a life richly attuned to the divine narrative, understanding that each day unfolds under the guidance of His sovereign hand.

### REFLECTIVE QUESTIONS

1. How does understanding **The Significance of Types and Shadows** enhance your perception of the continuity between the Old and New Testaments?
2. In what ways have you noticed **The Role of Numbers in Divine Communication** in your study of the Bible or your personal life?
3. How can **The Personal Nature of God's Messages** influence your daily decisions and interactions with others?
4. What are some challenges you face when dealing with **The Offensiveness of the Prophetic**, and how do you overcome them?
5. How does **The Imperative of Remembering** God's past deeds impact your current faith journey?

### ACTIONABLE STEPS

- **Cultivate** a deeper relationship with God by setting aside time each day to study prophetic symbols and their meanings in the Bible.
- **Equip** yourself with knowledge by attending a study group or class that focuses on the prophetic books of the Bible to better understand the context and application of prophecies.
- **Engage** in journaling your insights and revelations from Scripture, especially those that speak to you in a personal way, to track your spiritual growth and God's faithfulness in your life.

. . .

**JOURNALING Prompt**

Reflect on a recent situation where you felt God was speaking to you, perhaps through a type, a shadow, a number, or a direct scriptural insight. Write down how this message influenced your understanding or actions, and consider how you might be more attuned to such messages in the future.

# CHAPTER 8
# LAST WORDS

In conclusion, I can see throughout history that God has always been speaking. Therefore, it encourages me to always hear God speak in the right now and to have hope for what God is speaking about my future. Turns out we need to be really good at hope these days. Even as we look at the terrible tragedies of the past and the hopeful dreams of our future, our hope always has to be focused on Jesus and the heart of the Father. That really is His word. The prophetic is not just about telling the future, and it's not only about what's going to happen. The prophetic is about knowing the heart of the Father. Just because something terrible happens doesn't mean that God's amazing heart cannot be heard within it—in fact, that is one of the most important times when we need to be able to hear Him clearly. I hope that this book has helped you and will continue to help you to have this conversation with your friends, your family, your neighbors, and the people you come across. There will be times when you can say, "Hey, do you see this event over there? Well, the Kingdom of Heaven is just like that!"

## John 10:27 – "My sheep hear My voice, and I know them, and they follow Me."

In this chapter, I want to take you deeper into the rich tapestry of Scripture, where every figure, number, and story layers together to form a profound narrative about God's interaction with humanity. We begin by exploring **The Significance of Types and Shadows** in the Bible, which serve as more than ancient accounts; they are prophetic tools that God uses to communicate His eternal truths. These elements are not just historical; they foreshadow greater spiritual realities that manifest in the New Testament, offering a bridge that connects and enriches both the Old and New Testaments.

As we delve further, we see that **Understanding Prophetic Symbols** in Scripture is crucial. These symbols—whether water, fire, or bread—carry weighty meanings that are applicable not only in biblical times but also in our current context. They enrich our spiritual insight and biblical literacy, providing a deeper understanding of how God communicates His character and plans through seemingly ordinary elements.

Another layer of divine communication is seen through **The Role of Numbers in Divine Communication**. Scripture often uses numbers like 40, 12, and 3 to signify broader theological themes such as testing, government, and divine completeness. These numbers are meticulously placed within the Bible to reveal structured patterns and plans of God, illustrating His precision and meticulous attention to detail.

One of the most comforting aspects of divine communication is recognizing that **God's Persistent Voice Through History** has never waned. From the days of Abraham to the modern era, His voice remains consistent and clear. This continuity reassures us that the God who spoke then still speaks now and encourages us to listen for His voice in our everyday lives, making our relationship with Him an active and dynamic interaction.

Applying these biblical types and shadows to our lives shows their **Modern Applications of Biblical Types**. These ancient stories are not trapped in the past; they have direct implications for us today, guiding us in our spiritual and practical decisions. They help us see the relevance of Scripture in our daily lives, providing timeless wisdom that addresses modern challenges.

Each message from God is tailored uniquely to us, emphasizing **The Personal Nature of God's Messages**. God knows us intimately and communicates in ways that we, as individuals, will understand and respond to best. This personal approach not only highlights His love for us but also His desire for a personal relationship where He speaks directly into the circumstances of our lives.

However, engaging with God's word can sometimes be challenging, especially when we encounter **The Offensiveness of the Prophetic**. God's truth often confronts and challenges our comfort zones, prompting us to change and grow. It requires humility to receive these truths and allow them to transform us, which is a crucial aspect of walking in faith and obedience.

To effectively receive and act upon these divine messages, we must adopt **The Necessity of a Prophetic Posture**—an attitude of openness and readiness. This posture ensures that we are not passive recipients but active participants in God's plans, ready to move and respond as He reveals His will to us.

Furthermore, prophecy is not meant to be a distant or occasional experience; it should be part of our everyday lives. **Integration of Prophecy in Daily Life** means looking for God's voice in daily moments, using prophetic insights to guide our decisions and actions every day. This practice enriches our spiritual journey, making our daily walk with God more insightful and intentional.

Lastly, remembering **The Imperative of Remembering** God's past words and actions is vital. It builds our faith and provides a foundation for future trust. Reflecting on how God has moved in the past, both in Scripture and in our personal lives, encourages us to maintain our faith and trust in His promises, knowing that He is the same yesterday, today, and forever.

**REFLECTIVE QUESTIONS**

1. How have you experienced the personal nature of God's messages in your own life?
2. What symbols in Scripture have spoken to you most profoundly, and why?
3. How can adopting a prophetic posture change the way you engage with Scripture and prayer?
4. In what ways can you better integrate prophecy into your daily life to deepen your relationship with God?
5. How can remembering God's past actions and words bolster your faith in challenging times?

**ACTIONABLE STEPS**

- **Cultivate** a daily habit of listening for God's voice through Scripture reading and quiet reflection.
- **Equip** yourself with knowledge about biblical symbolism by studying different prophetic symbols found in Scripture.
- **Engage** in discussions with your faith community

about how God is speaking today and share insights to encourage others.

**JOURNALING Prompt**

Reflect on a recent situation where you felt God was communicating with you through your circumstances. Write about what you felt, how you responded, and what you learned about His character through that interaction.

# D DESTINY IMAGE

Destiny Image is a prophetic Christian publisher dedicated to empowering believers through Spirit-led messages. Our mission is to equip and inspire individuals to fulfill their God-given destinies by providing transformative resources that resonate with the Charismatic and Pentecostal faith.

We specialize in books, blogs, and back cover copies that reflect prophetic insights, dynamic teachings, and testimonies of faith. Our commitment to fostering spiritual growth and kingdom impact makes Destiny Image a beacon for those seeking to deepen their relationship with God and embrace their calling in the power of the Holy Spirit.